BÔ YIN RÂ
(JOSEPH ANTON SCHNEIDERFRANKEN)

THE GATED GARDEN
VOLUME TWENTY-SEVEN

WORDS OF LIFE

For more information
about the books of Bô Yin Râ and
titles available in English translation,
visit The Kober Press web site at
http://www.kober.com/

BÔ YIN RÂ
(JOSEPH ANTON SCHNEIDERFRANKEN)

WORDS OF LIFE

TRANSLATED FROM THE GERMAN BY
B.A. REICHENBACH

THE
KOBER
PRESS

BERKELEY, CALIFORNIA

For permission to quote or excerpt, write to:
The Kober Press
2534 Chilton Way
Berkeley, CA 94704

Email: koberpress@mindspring.com

This book is a translation from the German of
Worte des Lebens, by Bô Yin Râ (J.A. Schneiderfranken),
published in 1923 by Greiner & Pfeiffer, Stuttgart, and
Kober'sche Verlagsbuchhandlung Basel-Leipzig.
The copyright to the German text is held by Kober Verlag,
AG, Bern, Switzerland.

Printed in the United States of America

International Standard Book Number: 978-0-915034-20-8

Typography and composition by Dickie Magidoff

Book cover after a design by Bô Yin Râ

This translation is
gratefully dedicated to
Datti Schneiderfranken

In his book *Concerning Godlessness*, published in 1939, Bô Yin Râ included a chapter "Comments on the works belonging to my spiritual guidance *Hortus Conclusus—The Gated Garden—and its related writings*, in which he advises how to approach the individual works.

Regarding the present text he points out,

"Inner need compelled me to make *Words of Life* the title of a shorter book, which occupies as singular a place within my spiritual guidance as does *Worlds of Spirit*, if in a different sense. Eternal Life here speaks in solemn words of God to an awakening human soul, which in the end makes answer in a joyous vow."

CONTENTS

CHAPTER ONE

A CALL TO YOU

IN SEARCH OF ME YOU SET OUT ON YOUR quest, and now you ask, reproachfully and anguished, where I might be found.

My question to you, however, is why to this day you still have failed to find me?

Know this: To you I gave my seeing and my hearing, and on your tongue are the words of my language.

Why do you fall silent when I tell you to speak, while you know how to speak where only silence could grant revelation?

You fill deaf ears with empty words, and are enraptured by your senses' deceiving apperception, so that now my language appears to you foreign, and my words devoid of clear meaning.

Even so, you one day will have to answer me using my language, such as your lips had received it from me, when I let you depart from my presence.

You still attempt to hide from me behind a hedge of skillful words; but bear in mind that I am close to you, as light is to the lamp; and that from me you never can conceal yourself, although your eyes are unable to see me, as long as you let your own folly blind you.

What else do I want from you but that you find me? And, truly, finding me is easy.

I know that you are seeking me, even though you follow ways of error, and pretend your search is aimed at other things.

The fool is searching for me, no less than the sage; and the fool's way of searching is foolish only because he bars the way to me with obstacles, while the sage's foremost intent is making his path to me easier.

He rids himself of every burden, lays aside his clothes and his walking staff, that he may reach me naked, as he was born of his mother.

You, on the other hand, adorn yourself in garments of brocade; dress up in strings of pearls and precious jewelry; and heavy golden sandals you tie around your feet.

Then you ponder long and deeply, searching for the longest way, since to your mind only the longest way could be the right one to find me.

Thus oppressed by every possible burden, you wander endless roads, only to halt in the end from exhaustion, until your high-minded courage turns to hopeless despair.

Know that in this way you will never be able to find me.

You search in faraway distances, while I am closer to you than your own body, which, laden with gems, you intend to lead toward me, though truly I cannot think much of your jewelry, and the deceptive glitter of your garments merely conceals you from my eye.

Let all words of borrowed thinking rest, in order that my language be upon your lips.

Remain wherever you may be today, and rid yourself of every burden.

Make your way into your inmost self, naked and rid of all gems; and learn to keep silent, until my language returns to you, to bear witness of that which I am.

I loved you within myself when you were with me from times of eternity, and I love you still, despite your having left me.

It is not I who hides himself from you; it rather is yourself who seeks to conceal himself from me.

You let your eyes peer into empty space, assuming that you there perhaps might find me, while all you need to do is to return to yourself if you seek to be near me.

You still do not know that you hide yourself from me when you seek to conceal yourself from your own eyes behind the weighty robes of splendor in which you seek to approach me.

You do not know that I have given myself to you; and that all things you still search for outside of your being you never shall find—but within you.

Know this: the treasures of all worlds are merely dust beside the jewel you bear in yourself.

❧

CHAPTER TWO

MYSELF

I AM THE LIGHT THAT SHINES IN EVERY atom of your body.

This body, composed of solid and semi-sold matter, to me is like a lamp of alabaster, wherein all organs are illuminated by the light I am.

The body does not hold me.

Nothing is able to hold me.

Everything outside myself to me is merely the form of an image, and I am the light unto every form I pervade.

I am fluidic energy, and yet transcend fluidic energy of every kind.

I resound in all the harps and strings and flutes through the infinities of endless space.

I am the master of symphonies without number, whose echoes reverberate through the spheres of eternity.

Those who desire to know me, and would live in me through the power of light for all eternity, have to become one of my instruments.

In the brilliant chords of one of my symphonies must they resound through the infinite spheres.

I bind the sounds, and I dissolve them, according to my own inherent law, manifest within me from eternity.

As masters of my symphonies I have skillful musicians as players.

They all obey my signals, and none of them would ever play false notes upon my instruments.

I do no more than give the signs.

My musician then will cause the instruments to sound; and I again become the chord they thus bring forth.

Some of the instruments may grow aware, while others do not, that the sound they create is but the effect of my law; and that the chord resounding in them is myself.

The mortal remains you behold when you look at yourself from without are truly not what I am.

By means of that body, however, I have given my power a solid support, so that I may turn all things on this earth into sound, and as a chord bring myself forth in all things existing.

Beyond counting is the number of symphonies that lie dormant within me, yet would become manifest.

Into radiant sound do I want to transform myself in all things prepared to resound through my power.

Nor shall my musicians fail to help also you, if you want to become one of my instruments.

As a radiant sound shall also you eternally shine in one of my numberless symphonies.

It is I who can redeem you from bondage; for only when I myself resound within you will your bliss be eternal.

Recognize: the goal of all your longing is nothing other than to unify yourself with me in radiant sound.

Although you feel the longing that torments you heart, you cannot yet discern its cause.

Mute, as in a string that is not plucked, remains concealed your own eternal sound within you; but only if you will unite yourself with me shall you be able to bring your own sound forth within you.

A new chord then will sound unto the universe; and you shall apprehend your being, with me united in omnipotence, within your own eternal Self.

❧

CHAPTER THREE

TURNING INWARD

IT IS YOURSELF THAT YOU MUST LEARN to recognize if one day you would see yourself gain recognition.

You still pay attention to all kinds of voices within you, giving your name sometimes to one, and then to another.

Comprehend that you are something other than all the voices of visible reality, and something other than any voice of unseen spheres around you.

You still regard the things that you have taken on, but which you one day have to leave behind, as being your most personal possessions, so that they have to hide your essence from yourself.

You still pay attention to clamorous shouting around you, and thus can no longer hear your own words.

You also still seek me in all the clamor surrounding your ears on all sides; and listening with pain you expect to discover my words in that tumult.

Me, however, you cannot discern except in yourself; and only after you learned to discern your own being.

Not next to you, but in yourself am I concealed within you.

If, then, you truly desire to find me, do not search for me as being something outside of yourself.

For that would be a grievous folly and only should cause you to fall prey to phantoms of your own making, which you call forth when humbly you bow before a power that is not rooted purely in your own self.

Comprehend that I exist in all the spheres of cosmic space; and if like me you equally existed in every sphere throughout the universe, you there could find me also.

You, by contrast, find yourself at merely your own cosmic place.

No other can be by himself throughout the boundless universe where only you are by yourself.

Yet solely where you are alone with your own self can you discern your true being; and only after you have gained that self-awareness can I reveal myself to your perception.

It will be difficult for you to apprehend me in this way as long as you are still not able consciously to apprehend yourself.

It may appear to you that you might not be able to distinguish me from yourself if you were to perceive me within you.

You are too much in the habit of discerning only that which is outside of yourself; and so you are no longer able to feel what it means to discern things within you.

Truly, you have strayed a long way from yourself!

You still say "I," but that which uses this name has nothing to do with the true self you are.

At times it is your body and its instincts, at other times your links to the unseen part of the earth, which call themselves by that name, while the true self you are fails to assert its existence.

But in outer life you must learn to assert yourself, lest your external existence is to enchain you.

Be sure to keep all things external securely tied by the sturdy cords of your will, lest they fall upon you like a horde of bandits, which attack an unsuspecting traveler, tie him up, and plunder his possessions.

I gave myself to you—I, my own most precious gift—for, truly, I possess and can bestow myself; but you still do not know that you embody greater things within you than ever your imagination can conceive; for you have still not found yourself within.

All things that you believe in realms above you, you truly bear within yourself.

If only you were willing to teach your eyes, which still are gazing at the heavens, to turn their searching inward!

Learn to find your timeless self within your being's innermost, so that within yourself you can encounter me.

ℛ

CHAPTER FOUR

LOVE

T̲RULY, I HARBOR LOVE FOR MYSELF, AND YOU are to be my likeness, and love your own self more than anything else.

Not your physical body, nor whatever else in you might call itself "I," are you to love in this way "above all other things," even though bonds of love will always connect you to your body and the unseen energies within you.

"Above all other things" you are to love solely your own timeless self, in your innermost being —the self that you truly are, and wherein I dwell in concealment.

To love "above all other things" you ought to understand as meaning: more than everything that is outside to love the timeless self within you; and when you thus will love yourself, then only will you find your highest love—in me.

The teachings you received have thoroughly misled you if you were to think your love must be for everything.

Your highest love, which you can only find in me, once you have learned to love yourself, is free of any object kindling love; and some who fathomed only half the truth that can be known have thus concluded that it must encompass everything.

My love, however, only obeys my own inherent law and is confined within myself.

Everything it would encompass it needs to draw into myself.

Within myself, however, there is no will that does not want my being.

Thus should also you direct your love, when loving something in your outer life, with prudent choice.

"Not to love" you must by no means understand as meaning you should "hate."

There will be much your love shall not be able to embrace, but which you must by no means hate.

Free of either love or hatred you will need to confront by far the greater part of what you shall encounter in external life, excepting your own self.

You are to love whatever brings you to yourself, and thus to me.

Everything else should at all times remain deprived of your love.

But how could you know what you should love if you do not love your *self*—your timeless *self*, wherein alone your highest love is able to reveal itself?

Before you probed your own profoundest depth, and thus will love yourself "above all other things," all your love toward anything outside remains no more than semblance and deception.

You will deceive yourself when you before that time believe you "love"; and that which you pretend to "love," you have instead betrayed.

Then only will love have truly awakened within you when you have learned how to love your own self.

All who embodied love in its highest form have always embraced their being with love; have always imbued themselves with love's most radiant fire.

Be mindful, however, that even where you are not to feel love, you must still less give way to feelings of hatred, if in your highest love you seek to reach me.

Your ability to feel hatred should serve you as proof of your power to love; but not everything you feel capable of will help you to find your own self.

Love is the supreme affirmation of that which you love; not to love expresses negation. Hatred, however, is your admission of lacking the power to rid yourself of what you negate.

Whatever you negate you simply should regard as if, to you, it did not exist.

You should not want to see it any longer, and thus deprive it of the energies it constantly regains through your attention.

But if you succumb to hatred, you continue to feed what you hate with your own strength; and you will have to be careful, lest it become a monster, apt to devour you.

Those who truly were imbued with love, having found its highest form in me, were anything but spineless weaklings who lamely accepted whatever crossed their path; instead, they forcefully denounced abuses when they felt it necessary, but none of them ever surrendered to hatred.

In this way should also you endeavor to control your hatred; and if today you may not yet succeed, perhaps you will have mastered it tomorrow; if only you continue to be watchful, and resolved to raise yourself above it.

The more clearly you perceive that all your hatred merely nourishes the things you hate, the sooner shall you free yourself from falling prey to hatred.

Many a source of evil on this earth would long since have run dry if only hatred were not causing it again and again to overflow.

If you earnestly would see what is destructive to be consumed by its own self, you need merely to deprive it absolutely of your love.

As long as your "negation" continues to be active, you still have not negated in the real sense.

Whatever, in your judgment, ought to be negated must vanish altogether from your sight, and not in the slightest way gain your attention.

In this way you shall effectively deprive what you negate of its strength; and, liberated from all bondage, your love shall be able to affirm what it loves.

Within your highest love you then shall also find in me your highest affirmation, which in itself eternally loves solely its own being.

$\approx$

CHAPTER FIVE

ACTION

YOU LIE AWAKE YOUR ENDLESS NIGHTS, pleading that I hear your call.

Indeed, I know that you are calling me, and I gladly would rush to your aid; but you still reject my hand and keep waiting for help of a different kind.

I truly am the one you seek; but I am still unknown to you, and in my stead you want to find another; one who resembles what you have made of me by your mind's creative omnipotence.

Oh, that I were able to transform myself into the shape of your dreams, that you might recognize who is approaching you!

Yet I remain eternally immutable—at once my own inherent law, and equally that law's unchangeable effect—so that I stay forever who I am; far beyond the reach of all impulsive wishes that would change me.

It is for you to change the image that you shaped of me within your mind, where you are the creator.

Otherwise, you never shall know who I am; and so I would have to remain a stranger to you; I, who am closer to you than all others; for you conceal me within you.

You hide me from yourself, and then invent an idol, in which you imagine to find me.

Folly keeps you in bondage, while in yourself you possess measureless wisdom.

While it may be the folly of others by which you are bound, no one but you alone is able to sever those chains.

Before you are willing to know me such as I am, and have been in myself from eternity, you shall search for me in vain through all the spheres of creation.

All your longing desire will be of no use; for even if I respond to your plea and approach you, you regard me as a stranger, whom one passes without paying attention.

You first will need profoundly to alter the image you have invented of me for yourself, if it is to reflect my true features.

You will have to train your eyes to see in a different way if you want to behold me as I have been from eternity.

Comprehend: I am myself the strength of my law, and cannot desert my own being; even if my love for you could move me to release myself from that which I am, so that I might be your salvation.

But since I love you, I do not want your search in future to pursue mistaken paths; and thus you hear my voice today, as coming from a speaker whom you do not know.

I truly seek to be your *savior* and *redeemer*, but to this end you must yourself be willing that it be granted you according to my word.

You must forget all mental images before you can approach reality, which is eternal action; and everything conceived by your imagination you need to ignore as a baseless mirage.

You must finally learn to admit to yourself that your teachers did not know me, and thus proclaimed a welter of absurdities about me; for they regarded me as one of their kind; only much greater and mightier, not merely in holiness, but also in guilt; for if I were what they had conceived me to be, then such a construct of benighted speculation would, as his own opponent, eternally wage war against himself.

But I am forever at one with myself, being the ground of my own foundation, and nothing within me can oppose my own self.

Comprehend: I am consummate activity.

I am to myself both action's effect and intent.

I am my own cause and its consequence.

It is not the longing of your heart that lets you reach me on your search, or you would have found me long ago.

Only by being active will you find me within you; and no torment of longing through anxious nights shall reveal me to you as lucidly as will a conscious action that truly manifests your quest for me.

Do not assume, however, that it is your deed as such which causes you to apprehend my being.

You must of course consider the effects of your actions, and whether they can without question lead to success in your search, which is moved by your longing for me.

When thus you feel certain that your will pursues what is right, then hesitate no longer, and do not lose the inspired hour that finds you confident and ready to act.

Engaged in conscious action you then will in yourself encounter me, and be united with me in yourself.

In conscious action I want to experience my own self in you, whom I love.

In conscious action you are to serve me as witness and sign.

In yourself shall I thus perfect you; for only in me are you granted perfection.

Begotten of me, shall action be born then of you, that it continue to bring forth new actions, in accord with my own timeless will.

You shall yourself be born to me—and yours shall be a sacred birth—by virtue of your conscious, self-desired, freely chosen action, worthily performed by one who is in spirit truly free.

CHAPTER SIX

STRUGGLE

COMPREHEND: WHILE BEING ONE AND unified within myself, I nonetheless remain the cause of struggle without end.

Everything that would attain me can come to me only through struggle.

Solely having struggled shall you gain me, as the victor's prize.

I myself am never touched by any such struggle, for conflict within me cannot exist.

Whoever is still committed to struggle has not yet attained me.

But how can you find me within you unless you are able to conquer all things in yourself that will not let you discern me?

Without struggle you shall never overcome any of the obstacles blocking your path.

From this struggle you must emerge as victor, if I am not to remain beyond your reach forever.

This struggle will truly demand all of your strength and resilience.

It will be a struggle that calls for determined persistence.

It will be a struggle you must not tire to wage until victory is your reward.

You cannot prevail in this struggle unless you are resolved to draw upon all of your energies in order to force every obstacle barring your path into your service.

But in this struggle you must not seek to kill; for what you would destroy embodies energies that help you triumph in the end, once you have learned to bow them to your will.

Many already had sought to prevail in this struggle, but soon they lost courage, and then offered terms to all foes that opposed them.

Thus defeated they returned, and called out to all who wanted to enter the struggle, "It is not possible to gain victory in that strife!"

In every age, however, there were some who knew how to triumph; and crowned with the victor's evergreen laurels they returned from the field.

I want to see also you as a victor!

And so I give you this advice: as long as you still need to struggle, never forget that everything opposing you is only waiting for the moment when your will to gain victory shall abandon you.

No one engaged in this struggle was ever defeated who had not first been deserted by the will to prevail.

You may suffer setbacks more than once, but ultimate victory shall still not be denied you, as long as you do not irretrievably lose your will to gain victory; and that will is the faith in your triumph.

Every conflict, however, that breeds the impulse to kill, merely unleashes new conflicts; even if at first you appear to have triumphed.

Your aim, therefore, should not be to kill in this struggle.

The most dependable of your servants will become those in the end which your steadfast courage subdued in the struggle.

They now acknowledge you as their master, and shall willingly obey you in all perils.

With their support, your struggle will become a game, and nothing may any longer deny you victory.

But never forget that all these foes, which you are to transform into servants; no less than struggle and victory, as well as the field of the conflict, are exclusively found in yourself.

Even when you think you have to contend with external opponents, the truly decisive struggle will always take place in yourself.

You still are deceived by appearance, and constantly worry how you should meet the demands of external existence.

The things that here beset, and seemingly defeat you, are still ranked far too highly in your judgment.

You continue losing faith in yourself when anything in outer life compels you to retreat.

If only your eyes could see at last, to let you recognize that every victory in the outer world, no less than every external defeat, display no more than idle deceptions.

Only what in yourself you compel to obey and to serve you will in truth have been finally conquered.

Not until having gained victory in your own self, shall you in my eyes prove a victor.

Only this victory in your own self shall make me become the prize of your struggle.

I TRULY BESTOW MYSELF on no one who does not attain me as the prize after struggle.

Worthless, shallow, and gaudy trifles are all things that can be attained without struggle.

Everything of enduring worth shall become yours only by virtue of struggle.

Only your having struggled can earn you the victor's prize.

As a victor, however, I want to see you approach me, if I am to take note of your presence; and only with one not afraid of the struggle can I eternally unite my own being.

Have courage, then, and do not flee from the struggle which promises you a prize of such infinite worth.

∽

CHAPTER SEVEN

PEACE

Your soul is longing for peace; for the peace this world cannot give.

But that peace can become yours only after victory, gained in a struggle fought without fear; you thus shall long for that peace in vain as long as you dare not engage in such struggle.

Yet if you return to yourself in victory, nothing indeed shall disturb your peace any longer.

Many believe that ending the struggle would let them find peace.

Believing this is foolish; for the end of the struggle may prove your undoing, as long as you are unaware that one must never cease any struggle merely for the sake of having peace.

No one has ever successfully struggled for permanent peace who lacked the will to conclude the conflict only by having gained victory.

The longing for peace is a beguiling temptation; but pity the fate of those who succumb!

Such longing lets them become defenseless victims of their invisible foes, who subject them, unprotected, to their willful caprice, where even resistance without victory would have forced their enemies' weapons to serve them instead.

Thus, if you truly want peace, let nothing weaken your courage to keep up the struggle; and do not relent until your enemies offer you peace on their part.

Only then will you truly find joy in the peace you secured.

Until then, your weariness of the struggle will only mislead you to reach a deceptive peace; and what you assume to have achieved shall merely leave you the choice of either remaining the thrall of your foes forever, or to renew the struggle; and then perhaps to battle in a way that you may truly earn the victor's laurels.

You have often been given false counsel, being told that all who desired to find me needed to seek nothing other than peace.

But I wish to see vigilant warriors; and a peace that does not fall from destiny's tree like a ripened fruit is contemptible in my sight, and in truth merely folly; for I could more easily come to your aid had you succumbed in the struggle, than having abandoned the field for want of resolute courage.

The heroes who fought the great struggle, whose peace I became, were determined to fight to the last drop of blood in their veins; and, truly, they triumphed in victory, even though at times they may have appeared as merely the victims of their struggles.

And in no other way do I want to see you as well triumphant in victory, when your day has come.

In this way alone shall you find peace everlasting within me.

Peace, in my sight, is the certainty of the victor in battle, that nothing can henceforth challenge him any more to reopen the struggle.

Peace is solely that enduring inner calm, which is the prize of all battles, and the goal that fires their quest.

Peace is freedom from all need to engage in further conflicts.

Peace I regard as the power, gained in battle, to govern all former opponents and foes.

None but those who found such peace in themselves can then also find their peace everlasting in me.

For them I shall be the treasury guarding their peace.

In me they will find "the peace this world cannot give,"—the peace that is granted to only those, having prevailed in themselves, who then shall earn me as the prize of their struggle.

CHAPTER EIGHT

STRENGTH

IN VAIN YOU STILL SEARCH FOR THE strength that might help you to victory in your struggle, and to the peace enduring forever, in a realm far away, outside of yourself.

Also here the paths you pursue lead to error, and you are wasting your efforts on fleeting illusions.

You thus may search in vain throughout eternity, in all dimensions of infinite cosmic space, unless this day you wake up, and return to yourself.

Only within yourself shall you truly encounter me; but I alone am the One who gives himself to you, as the strength assuring your victory.

I am the strength that masters every power; for I am every power's activating force.

Be not deceived, nor harbor doubts about me, if you must see these powers as constant opponents.

In infinite configurations I release from myself powers in measureless number, into all worlds revealed as perceptions; and only through their opposition can they generate effects.

Dead and cold and eternally motionless would be the worlds that I forever set against my Being, as its outermost otherness, if the energies streaming from me through these worlds were not to remain at all times opposed to each other.

Within myself, however, I am the strength and life of all these powers, thus in conflict with each other; and within me they find their unity, no matter how fiercely they may differ in the aims they must pursue in the domain of physical perception.

Should one not call it foolish if you labor in strenuous servitude to make friends of particular powers, or seek to gain mastery over others by cunning and force, given that you could become lord and master of every power, if only you sought to find your own self in me?

Truly, you would laugh at anyone who, in the world of daily life surrounding you, were seen to act the way one sees you acting in the invisible dimension.

Yet nothing is holding you back; and even today you may wrest yourself from such folly; as soon as you want to awaken the will in yourself which no longer seeks anything other than to guide you in me, in your innermost self, to attain your perfection.

You then shall in yourself possess the strength in victory to triumph over all the forces of all worlds.

Within yourself you then shall witness all opposing conflicts unified.

You shall be able to control all energies that offer you resistance in yourself, by keeping them in such consistent interaction that their inherent opposition is retained, and yet will constitute a sacred unity.

Only when you shall have found yourself in me are you able to accomplish this wonder.

You then no longer are on either one side or the other, but in the inmost center of the strength which, from its essence lends all powers their effective force.

Only in me are you granted the certainty that unfailingly leads the will to gain victory to the goal of its quest.

Once you shall have found yourself in me, within your innermost, in union with my Being, no might in all the worlds can any longer frighten you.

No power then shall tear from you the victor's crown, not even hell itself; for that to which you give that name is no more than the inter-action of energies you now control.

❧

CHAPTER NINE

LIFE

YOU ARE A MYSTERY UNTO YOURSELF, AND you truly have reason to be.

You are aware of your existence, and bear within yourself your being's primal cause; but you still seek to discover your life's external origin and explanation in all things that forever shall remain outside yourself, and alien to your nature; although your search could let you find what you are seeking only if you were prepared to enter into your own self, and your profoundest depth.

For there I am myself the source of your existence; and nowhere but in me can you discern your being's final cause.

You are accustomed to speak of your *life* as if that "life" were a self-depleting energy that brought about your existence; but here you trust too much in what your eyes can see, and are misled by mere appearance; given that your body's mortal form appears to rise out of the night of non-existence, only to return again into the darkness of non-being.

What briefly sustains this visible form in existence, by error deceived, you considered your "life."

If error thus misleads you to assume that here you apprehend what is your "life," you truly have succumbed to a fateful delusion.

Profounder depths you need to probe within you, if ever you intend to reach your real life's eternal ground.

Learn to recognize above all else that your true *life* is nothing outside your own self; and comprehend that everything you know about yourself is merely knowledge based on the *effects* of what in you gains self-experience: as *life* that is itself its timeless ground.

Yet I am what in this way manifests itself within you as your life; and only after you have found me in yourself shall you be consciously united with your *life*.

Before that day you still believe what merely is *effect* to be the *cause*; since what you feel to be your "self" is merely the *reflection* of the life in which the timeless self-awareness of your being is granted you within me. For, be assured, as a gift I bestowed myself upon you, that through my strength you may discern yourself eternally rooted in me.

Seek to awaken your understanding, and to grasp that I am closer to you than all things you perceive as separate from yourself; I, whom you search for in vain in the outermost realms of existence; and since you do not find me there, you succumb to the delusion that you and your kind are not able to find me.

Many have thus been searching in vain through the farthest dimensions what had been too close to be seen by their eyes, which only explored the remotest horizon.

But to myself I remain: *Being* eternally in its own Self; and nothing not in me will my *Being* embrace; how, then, could you, whom I encompass, hope to encounter me, but in yourself?

Even that which to you is the outermost realm you perceive, to me is the innermost Self of my

Being; and you indeed would heap error on error if you assumed that in those infinite spheres your eyes explore to find me, I could not likewise be found by what in those realms owes existence to me.

But even as your mortal body cannot stay alive unless its lungs find air to breathe within itself; and as its presently existing form would promptly cease if it no longer *in itself* could use the air, by which this planet is enveloped in even its remotest regions, far from where your lungs draw breath, in that same way am I unable ever to unite myself with you, if you pursue your search for me outside yourself.

To you I am revealed as solely your own life.

In vain would you search through all spheres without end expecting to find me.

Within yourself alone am I the world that is yours.

When you speak of your "consciousness," you merely refer to the self-aware reflection of the luminescent atoms of your soul; comparable to the image of your body's inner structure, which the physician obtains on a screen of chemical substance, when he examines your body with the type of rays that will penetrate dense, material objects.

But even as the screen, which is to transform those rays into a visible image, must be prepared according to given requirements, that it will clearly display the true likeness of your body's inner structure in a luminous semblance, even so must also you prepare yourself, if you intend to become the mirror of your inmost self.

You shall not recognize me in yourself as your innermost life and being, before you have prepared yourself, with clearly awakened will, so that the atoms of your soul will lucidly reflect the image of your life to your own consciousness.

Then, however, you will find yourself united with me in this image; for what reveals its radiance in this way is truly my Self, as thus I experience my own life within you.

Enshrouded in darkness, even though my rays pervade it, remain to you all things that are not your own self.

Dark remains all that awakened will has not prepared.

Like the mysterious rays I mentioned above, I am indiscernible to the unprepared soul.

But once you have prepared yourself within your innermost, your light shall brightly shine forth in my radiance; and as your own eternal life will I reveal myself within you.

❧

CHAPTER TEN

LIGHT

INNUMERABLE KINDS OF LIGHT CAN YOU perceive in life on earth, yet every kind of light your eyes may ever see is far surpassed in luminous power by the incomparably brilliant light descending on this planet from that distant solar fire, whose radiant energy grants both the largest and the smallest thing on earth its form and structure.

Yet even this mightiest source of light that mortal eyes may apprehend would merely be a clouded glimmer if you compared it with the timeless Light which from the Spirit's heights may reach you, as soon as you are able to receive it.

It is no playful use of figurative images if you are told about the Spirit's Light.

What you are granted from the Spirit's realm in truth is real Light; and all external luminescence that can be physically perceived may be considered *light* in so far only as it imbues your soul with similar emotions as the primordial power, which reaches you from highest realms of Spirit, revealing itself as Light.

Concerning that Light, which shines "in the darkness," and which the darkness can never "perceive," one, whom I know as my own, once spoke to you as being "life"; and his words indeed proclaim the truth.

Those alone who found me in themselves, as being their own life, are also able to bear witness of that Light.

In its primordially begotten, all-embracing might shall this form of the Spirit's Light eternally illuminate your inmost being.

You shall yourself reflect the brilliance of that Light and of your radiance shall be no end.

Even as a skillfully polished diamond cannot reflect its inner fire unless it is suffused by physical light, so also can you not shine from your innermost, as long as you still love the darkness, and hide yourself from my sight;

from me—the Light that eternally flows from Itself, giving life unto all things existing, in radiant abundance, as a source without ceasing.

All that is dark you truly shall brighten with your own Light, once you will find yourself radiant in me.

All the wonders concealed in your being shall thus be revealed to you; and everything surrounding you will brilliantly reflect the Light you then embody.

Yet now you still are satisfied with staying in the dark, and merely harbor longings to behold the Light; even though vaguely aware that in its rays you might gleam, like a crystal suddenly struck by the light of the sun.

Or, if now and then you mean to overcome your lethargy, you are content with any ray of murky glow that reaches you, and will coax forth a dreary glimmer from your inmost self; a feeble flicker, which neither can enlighten you, and even less illuminate the darkness of the world around you.

All your capacity to shine you thus believe sufficiently proven in your judgment, only to find yourself once more in darkness, as soon as that feeble glow fades again in the distance.

You may display a cut of exquisite facets, and, conscious of your value, take rightful pleasure in your precious form; but never shall you in this way awaken to yourself within; and you will face yourself as a stranger, having nothing to say to yourself, as long as you let such weight and inertia restrain you.

The years of your life on this earth are rapidly passing, and every solstice shall find you at the place you stood before, groping in the same darkness, until fatigued your earthly eyes shall one day close forever, having seen the final rays of this material sun; but you, still fettered by your former darkness, will then no longer even see the physical image of the Spirit's living Light, which at least had appeared as a comfort to you in the depth of your inner darkness.

In vain shall you then attempt to awaken a feeling that even vaguely resembles what, in your mortal days, you at least could experience in the light of the physical sun.

Everything within you, and all your surroundings, while perfectly tangible, shall be veiled in profoundest darkness; yet nothing shall still your longing for Light.

For aeons living in harrowing night you then may well lament having wasted your life on earth; now a constant prey of chaotic experiences in hostile domains; until, in distant cosmic ages, you may at last perceive again the first faint ray of timeless Light.

One, who embodied the abundance of my Light, had for that reason once admonished you with this profoundly far-seeing word, "Work, while it is day; for the night will come when no one is able to work"—none who neglected to "work" when still alive; because for countless ages he then will be the victim of that darkness, which he had failed to escape during his earthly life; too readily satisfied, averse to effort, and deluded by the notion that self-experience aware of its worth was adequate wealth, so that he no longer had any need of me, the Light of radiant spiritual substance.

And thus I come to you, on this, your day on earth, because my love would see you tear yourself from suffering this fate: today, while you still have the power to escape it.

Once in bondage to the law prevailing in this realm, even I cannot release you from the chain of consequences it enforces; for I am the foundation of all law, and thus would be negating my own self were I to seek to set you free before your time has come.

Even if today, now that my word has reached you, you courageously wrest yourself from the bondage of darkness, you thereby act no less in accord with the law that is founded in me.

You alone have to decide whether the law you will follow is that which leads you to freedom, or the other, which holds you in bondage.

You have become the lord of your own fate at that unfathomably distant moment, when I —who eternally abide in the continuous present—let you depart from me, according to your will, to enter the journey you desired to take.

Before that event, you experienced yourself within me in conscious awareness of the state of continuous presence; comprising, as it were, the constant *horizontal* plane of all Being. After your departure, however, you were, and are able, if I am to employ this image, to experience no more than the *vertical plane* of all things existing; until the time when, be it according to the law of freedom, or that of bondage, you have found your way back again to where you departed—from within myself.

Profoundest secret insight is shown you in this image, and blest you are if you discern it.

Open your innermost, that echoes may there confirm what my words seek to tell you.

Within your innermost you thus will discover why ancient wisdom had told you about the abysmal "fall" that you suffered, when, from your highest perfection in me, you desired to probe the darkness beyond and below, which in this earthly existence surrounds you.

Yet even here, in this realm of your darkness, you still possess within you the strength to raise yourself to me, and to your former height.

You still retain the same inherent form, and are able to preserve it forever, such as I found you within me, when I was forced to let you depart, because the aim of your will no longer was height, but knowing the deep.

You still possess the power brightly to shine once more in me—the Light that embraces all light.

But you alone must make your will reverse its course, in order that at last—since aeons before you were born in an animal body on earth, you already had strayed through bewildering darkness—you now may find your way to the realm where the Light I am can reach you, so that for all eternity you may within me brightly shine anew.

Be mindful of this: I suffer in you; for within myself I cannot suffer, as in the radiance of my Light all suffering proves to be falsehood.

But I am truth everlasting; and whatever fails to find its fulfillment in me, is purely deceit and illusion.

That is why my call here comes to you, whose soul I love, so that you might forsake the falsehood disguising itself as suffering.

To that end I show you the way out of your darkness, so that in me—the Light everlasting —you might shine in radiant joy, before darkness may once again hold you in bondage.

In me you shall transform yourself into joy; and all the pain you suffered shall vanish without trace, like scars of wounds that healed, and then disfigure you no longer.

You must awaken in yourself as conscious joy; for I cannot reveal myself as Light within you until, transformed to joy, by your own will, you shall approach me.

That way alone will you, whom I treasure, find me within you as Light, in whose rays you then are to shine forever.

In joy shall you thus be transformed within me to the purest of Light.

❧

CHAPTER ELEVEN

TRUST

EVERYTHING YOU SEEK TO ATTAIN, YOU shall indeed attain, if you will trust my words.

Many things you already have sought to achieve, but failed to do so, because the ground of your trust was too shallow.

Your trust has to be anchored in the profoundest depths of your consciousness, so that no event you may encounter in life shall ever uproot it.

Like a tree that is to bring you precious fruits, you need to protect it, that the animals of the wild cannot gnaw at its trunk, preventing its growth.

All sapping shoots you must promptly remove, so that the trunk may draw its nourishment from all the richness of the ground, and not be deprived of anything it needs for gaining full-ness of strength.

But even when the tree defining your trust already has developed branches and twigs on a high and sturdy trunk, and its crown would unfold itself fully, you constantly will, as a good gardener, have to make certain that all excessive growth of twigs is carefully pruned, that the nutriments of the tree are not withheld from its nourishing fruits, so that it soon may bring forth a bountiful harvest.

If in the past you often had felt your trust came to nothing, I would say you merely had taken too little care that first your trust would grow profoundly in strength before expecting to harvest its fruit.

Being honest with yourself, you will have to admit that you made a "test," as it were, of your trust; and that you took a forced, willfully fostered feeling of almost stubborn determination to be the limitless trust of which you had heard it might grant you magical powers.

But playing with trust in this way is an act of presumption, and shall certainly not bring you blessings.

If you in truth would see the boundless trust I here describe take root in you, and steadily unfold itself, you carefully need to avoid all follies of merely wishing and assuming; for here it is *reality* that shall become effective; but this *reality* cannot give proof of its effectiveness as long as images of your imagination still occupy your inner world.

Know this: The trust that I would find in you obeys inexorable law; nor shall human willfulness be able so to change its workings that its effects would become manifest, as long as the demands of its inherent structure are not met—whether you are aware of your actions, or not.

Again, you surely will not see that boundless trust within you firmly rooted and developed overnight.

Like everything you intend to bring forth in your temporal form of existence, it will require its time of growing; and so you calmly will have to banish all impatient and untimely wishes, as they would only delay your advance.

Begin to awaken all energies of feeling you possess, and thus intuitively to discern what is to grow and form itself within you.

Once having sensed it, no matter how faintly, hold fast to what you were granted; and let all your thoughts be gathered in serving your high resolve: to protect the seed of what you experienced from suffering harm.

Let no day pass by without consciously recalling what you already are able to attain; and guard yourself against all thoughts of doubt, which, like a flock of birds, shall try to destroy the seedling before its roots could reach the depth of fertile ground.

Do not obstruct such roots' development, but loosen instead the soil of the Spirit within you; and leave it to the dew of grace that it may be pervaded by those subtle roots which are to nourish and increase your trust.

You thus will see it slowly grow stronger and stronger; and, as mentioned above, you need to take care that the animals of the wild shall not harm it, nor that sapping shoots deplete its strength.

Yet when in this manner your trust has fully developed its strength, you first will have to make certain that you indeed have grown the precious plant whose fruits you desire to harvest.

The only way you now shall gain such certainty is by calling upon your innermost to respond; and from that innermost will then the certainty rise in you that you truly may expect to harvest precious fruits—unless, that is, you had from the outset sowed only the drive of your untamed desires into your soil.

Until you receive confirmation, from your innermost being, that your trust offers promise of an exquisite harvest, wise restraint should prevent you from hoping for fruit.

Up to this point I have spoken to you only in images, but also without figurative language should be made understandable what here you need to comprehend.

Listen, then, and weigh within your heart:

What is to manifest itself within you is primordial energy.

This energy you can awaken only by virtue of the inner strength which human language designates as *trust*.

By no means should you now blindly trust that wishes of any kind shall always be fulfilled, as long as you merely keep trust in their certain fulfillment.

What is demanded of you is greater; and greater is what you are meant to attain.

I want you to trust me completely; and such absolute trust also includes that you shall leave the fulfillment of your wishes completely in my hands.

Only if you entrust the fulfillment of your wishes completely to me may you expect with absolute confidence that I shall seek to fulfill them.

Yet do not assume you need to tell me how they might best be fulfilled.

I alone truly know how they should be fulfilled, and whether fulfilling them would be for your best.

And I alone also know the way that will let your wishes find their fulfillment, provided they do not conflict with higher laws that govern within me.

Again, I alone know with absolute certainty when the time has been reached to grant your wishes fulfillment, if in my judgment, too, their fulfillment is welcome.

If you were able to gain fulfillment by other means, resorting to tricks and deceit, you may be certain that such fulfillment would finally prove your undoing, so that you would curse the day you attained it.

Put your trust in me, the way you ought to trust me—with confidence that has no bounds—and you may feel assured that I shall grant you everything that will prove beneficial to yourself and others.

Do not quarrel with me if my way of fulfilling runs counter to what you expected.

Do not quarrel with me if I do not fulfill what to you seems so easy to grant; nor if I, instead, let your wishes encounter the very opposite of what you consider "fulfillment."

Patiently wait for events to unfold; and then only judge whether I acted in your best interest, or, for your own good, brought about different things, in order thereby to attain your wishes' ultimate goal of longing.

Absolute trust in me is a pledge that you will not deny me your trust, even if my way of pursuing your aims does not, in its wisdom, accord with what you expect.

❧

CHAPTER TWELVE

ILLUMINATION

WITH LIGHT DO I WANT TO IMBUE your soul—I, who experience myself within you, being radiance eternal ablaze in all light.

Out of my radiance alone can you be granted illumination; nor is there any light you may find outside of yourself that could truly illuminate your whole being.

All light you perceive outside your own self comes into being through me; but I am hidden within your innermost; and from your innermost only can my Light make you shine.

You that hide in darkness, comprehend: I am myself all Light; I am the radiance in all light; I am illumination unto all who long for me within them.

I have shown you manifold paths you need to pursue to the end if you seek to attain me.

Not that everyone needs to follow the selfsame path; but all shall recognize some of those I have shown you as clearly their own, so that they can no longer feel uncertain whether they are on the path that leads them to me, or had trusted instead illusive mirages, which lure them ever more deeply into deserts of phantoms.

Yet if, with inner constancy, you have pursued the paths you recognized as those for you to follow, you most assuredly will, at the end of one of those paths, at last encounter me; then shall the day have come on which I can illuminate your inner being, so that everything that had before been darkness in yourself, must now transform itself, and shine in radiant brightness in my Light.

Illumination means: making all things visible that once had lain in darkness, prevented from being perceived.

Illumination means: shedding light on all the hidden corners in the house of the soul, and thus leave no more hiding places where you might encounter vipers and venomous toads.

Illumination finally means: flooding the house of your soul with light of such brightness that its luminous rays penetrate far into the valleys of darkness and all the unwholesome creatures of night will be frightened, and flee to their lairs.

You have often believed that you could see quite clearly in the hazy light you received from the earth, to whose laws your own free will has condemned you to bondage.

The light of the intellect then seemed to you shining brightly; and whatever it sought to illuminate you judged to be so clearly displayed that you no longer felt need for light of more radiant brightness.

You one day shall become aware that everything your intellect had until now displayed so very clearly, as you confidently had assumed, in truth still lay profoundly concealed in darkness; for while you perceived the contours, you could not fathom the least of that which their outline embodies.

It seemed to you a given fact that any light your senses can perceive could only shed its rays on objects from without; yet now you shall become aware that you are capable of learning to see in my Light, so that whatever you perceive must equally reveal to you its innermost nature.

In truth, it is not something trivial you are meant to attain when, by grace of Love, by Action and Struggle, at last you found Peace, and Strength, and Life within me—who is the Light in you that shall illuminate your soul forever.

There have been not a few that sought to find illumination before they had taken, and reached the end of the paths, which alone could have led them truly to Light.

But thousands of phantom lights were lying in wait on their paths; and so they fell prey to the one that most subtly beguiled them, believing they were "illuminated," while being more deeply immersed in darkness than all those merely searching aimlessly, because they recognized the falsehood of deception, but could not find the path they were meant to pursue.

But those who even dread to enter, and make their way to the end of the paths they need to pursue if they long to encounter me, in radiance to shine in my Light, they in truth are not worthy of illumination, but deserve in desolate night to grope things like dreamers, instead of beholding them clearly in me—as only in me one can ever behold: penetrating all things that exist; for only in me could all things existing come into Being; and I carry all Being within me, even as a mother bears her body's fruit.

Those who seek illumination before making themselves worthy deserve to be mocked by phantoms; for they confuse reality with their illusions, so that it is no more than just if they accept illusions as "reality."

How crowded, sadly, is this life on earth with those deceived by their own baseless notions!

And how consistently have they obstructed every gate through which they could be reached by one who might still rid them of their fantasies!

I truly do not want to see you among the flock of those who deceive themselves; and thus I counsel you, whose soul I love, because in you I have my tabernacle: Do not flee the paths that seek to lead you to me; even if they often may seem dark and comfortless; for be aware that I am like the sun, and thus my Light shines never more brightly than after dark clouds had kept it hidden from mortal eyes.

Also to those seeking shelter in darkness am I their innermost Light, and my sacred shrine is within them; although they bury it beneath heavy shrouds and search to find outside what only in their innermost is able to reach them.

Proud in their vain presumption, they deem themselves able to find within themselves the Light that could illuminate their being, without the guidance of helpers, whom I myself have created from their own kind, so that through them my Light be transformed to a brightness which those still in the depth of night can yet endure; lest the rays of my Light, surpassing the blaze of the sun, should injure their eyes so severely that they would never again be able to see.

The sun itself, none can approach; but all may receive its light; and even though millions may share it, each one is granted abundance; nor would anyone gain more if the sun were to shine on no other.

But first its rays must pass through manifold layers of cosmic space, before they are at last transformed within the planet's atmosphere, so that your eyes are able to endure them.

If you were able to approach them where they depart from the sun, you surely would be instantly annihilated in their fire.

You doubtless also would consider anyone a fool who seriously believed the light of the sun could reach him, even if between him and the radiant stellar body no substance of any nature existed, which served the light's vibrations as a medium enabling motion.

Yet something similar expect all those who seek to find me within them, before having opened themselves to the circuit of spiritual energy I have formed for myself, through some of their kind, as a substance transforming the rays of my Light.

While you truly bear me within you, and though I am closer to you than even your temporal body, only your consciousness can reveal my presence within you.

Your consciousness, however, is limited in many ways, and would never be able to grow aware of me, had I not generated, in some who live on earth like you as human beings, a transforming energy, whose overflowing waves proceed from them, and thus are made accessible to every human consciousness, provided it will strive toward that transforming power, by virtue of its life and deeds.

For thousands of years have I thus become known to the consciousness of humans on earth; and as long as human beings shall live on this planet, there will always be some in their midst whose spiritual nature will serve me to engender this transforming power.

Yet even if among all human beings there were ever only one in whom I could create it, since of his own free will he had offered himself for this task, long before his life in an earthly body, through this single one alone the consciousness of every human being would still receive that energy of transformation; for what I thus bring forth in even one of their number is not confined by any means to him alone, but manifests its essence in vibrations that spread across all regions of this globe, thus creating similar reverberations in every consciousness that knowingly, or following its intuition purely by faith, longs to find me with every fiber of its soul.

Those whom I have, since ages immemorial, through all generations, continued to bring forth to serve me as my Luminaries, were nearly at all times committed to live unrecognized, strictly secluded from the distractions of mundane concerns; very seldom only had one of them been called upon to perform his task also while living among others, in public.

Only when the fullness of time demanded new seed to be sown, which would sprout in my Light, did I sanction that call.

Yet one thing is the energy of transformation, which continuously I generate in those who became my Luminaries, and something different again is the work in the visible world, which I at times call on one of them to perform.

No other, however, but one of these Luminaries could ever fulfill the demands of such work.

What you receive from one performing such work, you ought to consider as guidance, which may teach you how to prepare yourself for your quest; but the source that lends you the ability to find me within your own self, you should recognize as being purely the energy of transformation, which I continuously generate in each one of my Luminaries, whether he performs his work in the midst of the world, obedient to his vow and calling, or were to live in strictest seclusion, beyond the reach of any human contact, having no other task than to direct the energy, which I create in his spiritual nature, whence it flows forth, being able to reach the sphere of consciousness of all humankind.

Here you should not attempt by the mind's gloomy lantern to shed light on what will become lucidly clear only when it unfolds itself in your own life's experience.

Yet bear in mind that many thousands have sought, but never found me, as mired in dreams of physical consciousness, they entangled themselves too much in the snares of their own self-sufficiency, so that the thought of asking for help to be granted illumination had become inconceivable; and so they were no longer able to "knock" at the gate that is unlocked without delay to all who know how to "knock."

Thus, if you seek illumination, open wide your heart, and create within yourself the readiness of a soul that desires to be given what it still does not possess.

Act like someone who knocks at the door of a treasury, knowing he is entitled that the door will be opened.

But do not attempt to enter the portal with counterfeit keys, like a thief; nor, like a soldiering looter, to batter it down by force.

You would not succeed in either attempt, but fall asleep from exhaustion in front of the door, where deluded by mocking dreams you would fancy that you had entered.

Likewise, be careful never to take before you are given!

Here, too, you would never be able to grasp what you think you are seeing before you; and every effort to seize what you desire would only allow you to grope empty air.

But if you resolve to let my words be your guide, your fruitless search shall soon have an end.

Fulfilling the law that here requires fulfillment, you shall know how to find.

Opening your heart to the wellspring of grace, which is not moved by willful whim, you are to find illumination that shall forever grant you timeless Light.

❧

CHAPTER THIRTEEN

AVOWAL

O, TIMELESS ONE, TRANSCENDING ALL com-prehension; primordial Wellspring of might, sending the radiant stars of Your Word into my night of unknowing: Let my gratitude like clouds of incense rise in Your sight, imbuing Your temple's boundless infinity!

In truth, I do not know how to address You, unless Your Name were—hallowed by Your Being—the same I learned to give myself, when I awaken to my being and say "I."

YOU, primordial " I," primordial Light, primordial Word are the primordial Ground of my being.

As the image and likeness of Your Name have You taught my soul to give me my name.

Even though darkened through all the barriers of my own making that were to conceal You, Your Light has been able to reach me.

As *Lucifer*, a bearer of Your Light, had I once been near You, before I caused myself to fall into the depths of night and its horrors, when I presumptuously believed myself to be the LIGHT.

You now bring forth, through beings of my kind, in order to release me, the incomparably sublime transforming power of Your Love, so that in me—arising from the virgin nature of the soul—"CHRIST", the Lord, Your WORD, is able to be born, to wrest me from the agonies of hell, and darkness far beyond all hope of Light, to guide me back to You.

You, the primordial Ground of my being, reveal Yourself to me. In human words You teach me how to find You. You show me that in You abides eternal Grace, which, far removed from willful whim, is timeless Law that must be met; for only thus can Grace approach my soul.

How very far from You were those, indeed, who told me about "grace," as if, like persuadable mortals on earth, You could release me from guilt, or let it weigh upon me, according to Your mood and temper.

Now You have come to me Yourself to instruct me; and I recognize You, even though my eyes are still dazed by the blinding clarity of Your Light.

Now I know that I am solely the image of Your Life; and that all things I once had ascribed to myself were purely effects of Your all-empowering Might.

Toward You, my innermost being, shall henceforth my soul be turned!

In You alone can it rest, securely protected.

Only from You may it expect its salvation.

From You alone can rescue come to release it.

Had I only recognized sooner how I could have found liberation, and had not constantly searched for "redeemers to come," while in my own self I bore You, the timeless Redeemer.

Yet now I truly will not grumble, nor bemoan my fate.

This is the day on which I was granted salvation.

Praised be forever the day and the hour when You, my Innermost, turned Yourself toward me!

I could not ever escape from Your sight, even though never wanting to turn to You.

Though shrouded by night, and losing myself, I still would continue to be, even unknowingly the distant reflection of the wonder surpassing all wonders, which You remain throughout eternity.

But now that You called me Yourself, I truly shall not fail to heed Your call!

How many years have I not patiently longed to receive Your call!

You that sustain my soul within You: O guide me henceforth by that energy of transformation You bring forth in human vessels of the Spirit, that I may knowingly behold, like those whom You prepared to be Your helpers to save me.

This is my vow: To You alone I belong; nor is there a thing within me that still might claim part of my being.

I am solely Your own, and no longer call mine anything that would not be offered to You!

In You alone do I long to find my salvation and bliss without end!

To You alone shall now every breath I draw serve as a hymn of praise without end!

You alone shall become the center of all my thinking!

By Your grace alone do I desire to be, in days to come, alive in Life everlasting!

YOU
THAT
I AM.

REMINDER

"Yet here I must point out again that if one would derive the fullest benefit from studying the books I wrote to show the way into the Spirit, one has to read them in the original; even if this should require learning German.

"Translations can at best provide assistance in helping readers gradually perceive, even through the spirit of a different language, what I convey with the resources of my mother tongue."

From "Answers to Everyone" (1933), *Gleanings*. Bern: Kobersche Verlags-buchhandlung, 1990

Within Bô Yin Râ's cycle of thirty-two books
called *The Gated Garden*,
these three books form the central core
and are meant to be read together:

The Book on the Living God

Contents: Word of Guidance. "The Tabernacle of God
is with Men." The "Mahatmas" of Theosophy. Meta-
Physical Experiences. The Inner Journey. The En-Sof.
On Seeking God. On Leading an Active Life. On "Holy
Men" and "Sinners." The Hidden Side of Nature. The
Secret Temple. Karma. War and Peace. The Unity
among Religions. The Will to Find Eternal Light.
Mankind's Higher Faculties of Knowing. On Death. On
the Spirit's Radiant Substance. The Path toward Per-
fection. On Everlasting Life. The Spirit's Light Dwells
in the East. Faith, Talismans, and Images of God. The
Inner Force in Words. A Call from Himavat. Giving
Thanks. Epilogue.

The Kober Press, 1991. 325 pages, available in hardcover, paperback, Kindle, and other eBook formats.

This work is the central volume of the author's *The
Gated Garden*, a cycle of thirty-two books that let the
reader gain a clear conception of the structure, laws,
and nature of eternal life, and its reflections here on
earth. The present work sheds light on the profound
distinction between the various ideas and images of
"God" that human faith has molded through the ages
—as objects for external worship—and the eternal
spiritual reality, which human souls are able to experience, even in this present life. How readers may attain

this highest of all earthly goals; what they must do, and what avoid; and how their mortal life can be transformed into an integrated part of their eternal being, are topics fully treated in these pages.

What sets this author's works on spiritual life apart from other writings on the subject is their objective clarity, which rests upon direct perception of eternal life and its effects on human life on earth. Such perception is only possible, as he points out, if the observer's *spiritual* senses are as thoroughly developed to perceive realities of timeless life, as earthly senses need to be in order to experience *physical* existence. Given that authentic insights gathered in this way have always been extremely rare, they rank among the most important writings of their time, conveying knowledge of enduring worth that otherwise would not become accessible

The Book on Life Beyond

Contents: Introduction. The Art of Dying. The Temple of Eternity and the World of Spirit. The Only Absolute Reality. What Should One Do?

The Kober Press, 2002. 167 pages, available in hardcover, paperback, Kindle, and other eBook formats.

This book explains why life "beyond" is not so much a different and wholly other life, but rather the continuation of the self-same life we live on earth. The difference between the two dimensions lies chiefly in the organs of perception through which the same reality of life is individually experienced. On earth we know that life through our mortal senses, in life beyond it is perceived through spiritual faculties, which typically awaken after death. At that transition, the human consciousness, which usually is unprepared for the event, is at a loss and finds itself confused by the beliefs and concepts of its former mortal life. As a result, the new arrival faces certain dangers; for, owing to these mental prejudices, the person is unable to distinguish between perceptions of objective truth and the alluring phantom "heavens" generated by misguided faith on earth.

To help perceptive readers form correct and realistic expectations, that they may one day reach the other shore with confidence and without fear, this book provides trustworthy guidance into spiritual life, its all-pervading structure, laws, and inner nature. Given the unbreakable connection between our actions here on earth and their effects on life beyond, the book advises how this present life may best prepare the reader for the life that is to come.

The Book on Human Nature

Contents: Introduction. The Mystery Enshrouding Male and Female. The Path of the Female. The Path of the Male. Marriage. Children. The Human Being of the Age to Come. Epilogue. A Final Word.

The Kober Press, 2000, 163 pages, available in hardcover, paperback, Kindle, and other eBook formats.

Together with *The Book on the Living God* and *The Book on Life Beyond*, *The Book on Human Nature* forms a trilogy containing guidelines toward a new and more objective understanding of both physical and spiritual realities, and of the human being's origin and place within these two dimensions of creation.

The Book on Human Nature at the outset shows the need to draw a clear distinction between the timeless spiritual component present in each mortal human, and the material creature body in which the spiritual essence is embodied during mortal life. The former, indestructible and timeless, owing to its being born of spiritual substance, represents the truly human element in what is known as mortal man. The latter, physical, contingent, and subject to decay and death, is no more than the temporary instrument the spiritual being uses to express itself in physical existence. Given that the spiritual and animal components within human nature manifest inherently discordant aspects of reality, they typically contend for domination of the total individual. Experience shows that in this conflict the animal component with its ruthless drives and instincts clearly proves the stronger.

To help the reader gain a realistic understanding of the human being's spiritual and physical beginnings, by way of concepts more in keeping with humanity's advances in every discipline of natural science, the book explains, to the extent that metaphysical events can be conveyed through language, the timeless origin and source of every human's spiritual descent. It likewise shows that the material organism, now considered mankind's primal ancestor, existed long before it was to serve the spiritual individuation as its earthly tool. In this context the author points out that the traditional creation story, such as it has survived, is not simply an archaic myth, invented at a time that lacked the benefits of modern knowledge, but instead preserves, in lucid images and symbols, a truthful view of actual events. Events, however, that did not happen merely once, at the beginning of creation, but are a process that continues even now, and will recur until this planet can no longer nurture human life.

Even so, the principal intention of the present work, as well as of the author's other expositions of reality, is not so much to offer readers a new, reliable cosmology, but rather to encourage them to rediscover and awaken the spiritual nature in themselves, and thus to live their present and their future life as fully conscious, truly human beings.

⁖

THE KOBER PRESS

www.ingramcontent.com/pod-product-compliance
Lightning Source LLC
Chambersburg PA
CBHW022153080426
42734CB00006B/422